You Can Be Happier Now

By John Doherty
Copyright 2015 John Doherty

TABLE OF CONTENTS

John Doherty

<u>DEDICATION</u>

This book is dedicated to Nancy for her prodding, her reading, her suggestions, her hard work to make it a reality. Without her, this book would not be.

To all those I love and to all who share this journey from birth to inevitable death.

Let's enjoy the journey.

Cover illustration by Rosalinde Block   www.rosalindeblock.com

Cover design by Caligraphics

INTRODUCTION

HAPPINESS IS A LEARNABLE SKILL

The purpose of this book is to spread some knowledge about how to live more happily. It is intended as a beginning, not a list of answers. It is meant to make you think. About whether your happiness is acknowledged as **the** major priority in your life. About what skills you can work on to improve your happiness. About the answers that have worked for me. I hope that in your Journey you will find answers of your own

The book is divided into four sections:

Section One: The Beginning

How it all began and the answers I found.

Section Two: The Eight Steps and my Journey

This section contains a brief meditation on each step followed by the Journey that took me to its creation. It is a nudge to make you think about your real goals; about how you live and why. About whether your life could be happier (and whose couldn't?).

The Journey portion is the story of how my ideas of happier living developed. How I got to the path I now tread. If you read one Step each day and think about it during the day your ideas about life will expand. Your thoughts about how each Step applies to the circumstances in your life will open the door to living more happily.

Section Three: Happiness.

We need to know what happiness really is before we begin our search for it. Why making happiness **the** major goal in your life is not selfish or self-centered as we have been taught but is the only correct approach to living. It results in a life that will lead to ethics that promote our own happiness as well as that of others. Concentrating on our personal happiness will lead us to help create a caring and just society for all. There are many ideas about

4

John Doherty

happiness and how it can be achieved. Many of them are incorrect. This Section presents some of the ideas and points out why I agree with some and disagree with others. Finally, the Section provides my own ideas about the happiness we all want so much.

Section Four: Joysongs.

Joysongs is a series of aphorisms that I have found helpful in living more happily and my meditations about them. Perhaps you will find them helpful, too. I'm sure you will be able to add many others. I'd appreciate hearing any you think might be useful.

THE BEGINNING

"Each man is as happy as he makes up his mind to be." A. Lincoln

"Happiness is the whole aim and end of human existence." Aristotle

Happiness is no accident. It is the inevitable result of using certain principles in daily living.

Some happy souls absorb a few of these principles from their family as they grow up. The acceptance of even one or two of these principles is so powerful that it produces those people we think of as "naturally" happy. The lucky few, we tell ourselves, who are born that way.

In 1984, 1 stumbled on the first of the Principles of Happy Living.

It was an incredibly miserable year. I had lost my job, filed bankruptcy, my wife left me, and my father died. I was 47 years old and for 47 years I had done my best to follow the "rules" and live a good life. But I was unhappy.

As I considered my misery, I realized that I could accept my unhappiness or l could fight it.

By accepting that my unhappiness was my own responsibility, I no longer blamed others or circumstances. Just me.

That decision changed my life. It started me on the search for rules of living that would result in a happier life.

The only time to start on the search for a happier life was "Now." No preconditions. No "I'll be happy if I can get ...." or "When he does........". None of that. I would learn to be happy with what I had. With things the way they were, not the way I wanted them to be.

My search for a happier life began with religion. I first looked more deeply into Christianity. I studied other religions and the philosophies of Buddha, the Tao, and Zen. I practiced meditation and contemplation.

Aristotle, Epictetus, Seneca, Nietzsche, Hobbes, Mill, Emerson and many others had studied and written about happiness. Modern thought stimulated by the psychological and sociological revolutions since Freud also had much to offer about how to live happily. The Twelve Step Recovery Programs offer a method of happy living as well as recovery from addiction. I incorporated some of the principles I found in them, too.

My searching was not in vain. From my study I realized that the great teachers drank from a common stream. The stream of truth has been revealed to us, forgotten, then rediscovered again and again. The rules of how to live are no secret. Many have preached the Way.

But, as humans, we seek easier ways. Short cuts that will avoid the hard work required. We often seek to find happiness in money, or pleasure. But we cannot.

Over and over, mankind has been shown how to live happily. Over and over he has forgotten.

Religion, psychology, and philosophy all have common themes. Happiness is the goal of man. Certain ways of living will result in happier lives. I found that Eight Principles of living happily were spread among the great teachers. These Eight Principles, if learned and practiced constantly, will result in a happier life.

I distilled these eight principles into Eight Steps and by practicing them began a successful journey. I found that happiness is not due to chance but is a skill that can be learned just as any other skill. It requires only two things: study, and then practice.

Simple to understand but very difficult to live, the Eight Steps become easier with time and practice. With the encouragement of success, they will become second nature.

My Journey

Each life is a fantastic and often frightening Journey from birth to death. This is the story of my Journey and what I learned about living more happily. As each of us treads this path, we make mistakes. Some of us welcome these "mistakes" and learn from them. There are some unfortunates who repeat them and expect the result to change.

Research has shown that examining our mistakes is the best way to learn. We will continue to be offered more of these opportunities than we might like, but using them to learn will increase our skill at this job called "living".

This is a story about learning and my mistakes. How I looked to the wisdom of the past to find answers to the problems I had in the present. To study religions and recent scientific studies about how the mind works to learn about happy living.

The common principles I found changed my life.

Progress was not an even path. I stumbled, then raced ahead, then trudged slowly along. But I continued to learn, to practice, and to improve how I lived my life. As time went by, I got happier. Progress has been, if not steady, at least reliably forward toward my goal.

The First Step in my journey to a happier life was a gift. Somehow, grace of God or pure luck, I realized and slowly came to accept that I alone was responsible for my happiness. Gradually the other Seven Steps were revealed and discovering each of them was a process that took place over years. As each step was revealed and I made it part of my life, my life improved. The process is continuing.

These Eight Steps have become the basis of how I live. The Steps contain wisdom selected from the writings of the giants who preceded us as well as current research. With time, practice, and the rewards the Steps provide, I have become more proficient at living happily.

John Doherty

I want to share what I have learned so others will also be able to live happier lives. Even those who see happiness as a goal beyond their reach can live more happily.

I am not happy all the time. Even now, after 30 years of effort, there are days when I wake up and the world seems dreary and gray. Sometimes I allow things to get me down. But when that happens, I look at the Eight Steps and almost always find that I am neglecting one or another or maybe a few. By concentrating on them for a few minutes I can return my world to a happy state.

Living happily is a learned skill. It is a skill just as cooking, playing golf, or driving a car is a skill. As with any skill, it takes practice to become proficient. How to live more happily is the most important skill you can develop. To learn it, first you study, then you practice, then you live it. The longer you practice, the better you will get.

Then happiness will become a habit.

THE EIGHT STEPS TO HAPPIER LIVING

These are the Eight Steps I took that changed my life. Perfection in using these steps is not the goal. I have not achieved that goal and I never will. But the attempt has enabled me to improve and provided the reward of a happier life.

1. **Accept complete responsibility for your happiness**

2. **Accept what you cannot change, especially other people.**

3. **Live in the present enthusiastically and honestly.**

4. **Want what you have.**

5. **Control your negative emotions, particularly anger.**

6. **Participate in a group that will provide the benefits of community.**

7. **Meditate, it feeds your spirit.**

8. **Practice, practice, practice.**

CHAPTER ONE

STEP ONE

ACCEPT COMPLETE RESPONSIBILITY FOR YOUR HAPPINESS

As with any journey, the first step is the most difficult. It is also necessary if we are to take control of our happiness. We must admit that we alone are responsible for our happiness. Not circumstances. Not others. Just ourselves.

We are all reluctant to give up the ease and comfort of blaming circumstances or others. By allocating blame outside ourselves, we excuse ourselves from the effort of changing.

Responsibility means accepting the consequences of our actions. But when we accept responsibility we also assume control. One cannot be held responsible for things that are beyond their control. If we deny responsibility, we forfeit control.

As soon as we assume responsibility we are able to begin making changes. Immediately. Without waiting for any change in others or circumstances. The only one who must change is me, the one person in this world over whom I do have control.

I am responsible for all my choices. By accepting that responsibility I gain control over my happiness and the freedom to be who I wish to be.

Question:

Is that thing that prevents you from being happier really the cause or just an excuse?

Sayings:

"Responsibility is a prize to be claimed, not a duty to be avoided."

"If you deny responsibility for something then you are powerless to change it."

John Doherty

MY JOURNEY TO STEP ONE
ACCEPT COMPLETE RESPONSIBILITY FOR YOUR HAPPINESS

My Journey began in earnest that day I finally accepted that I was responsible for the happiness in my life or the lack of it. With this acceptance came the realization that I could be responsible only for something over which I had control. I will not be arrested if you rob a bank. By admitting responsibility, I also accepted control. The knowledge that I had the power to change my life was almost overwhelming.

I felt very fortunate to come to the conclusion that my happiness was completely my own responsibility.

It was not an easy concept to accept. There was a two year struggle before I fully accepted that my unhappiness was my own fault. I would seize on any excuse to blame circumstances, others, or luck for my unhappiness. But I knew that I was copping out and that the only one who had control and was responsible for my happiness or lack of it was me.

It was obvious that there were some circumstances where accepting complete responsibility was not true. If I were starving I would not be happy. If someone was hitting my hand with a hammer I would not be happy. If I were forced every day to do things I didn't want to do, I would not be happy. Where could I draw the line and not leave myself that dangerous crack through which I would blame circumstances or others for my unhappiness?

I knew that once I accepted some wiggle room I would expand it. The line would shift, then shift again, until I was blaming children, lover, boss, money, recognition, health, or anything else I could stretch to fit within my ever expanding boundary of blame.

How could I set a line that would prevent me from shifting the responsibility away from myself where I knew it belonged?

On the Fourth of July I was driving along listening to NPR when the answer came. In celebration of Independence Day, someone was reading the Declaration of Independence. I heard "We hold these truths to be self-evident, that all men are created equal, that they are endowed by their Creator with certain unalienable rights, among these are the right to LIFE, LIBERTY AND THE PURSUIT OF HAPPINESS."

Thank you Thomas Jefferson! Of course! That was the answer that I had been seeking. The necessities of life and the freedom to think and speak as I wished were all I needed in order to control my happiness. My rule became "I am responsible, once the necessities of life are satisfied".

I used to work in a shop that hired young people for the summer. It was interesting to watch their development as they returned summer after summer. Some learned and matured. Some I learned from. One young woman, Debbie, taught me a lot.

She was a Junior in High School the first year she worked at the shop. One time she was complaining about how unhappy her life was. I asked her why she was so unhappy. She said, "Of course you're happy. You have lots of money and only work because you want to."

I explained her error and that I worked because I needed the money to support myself. Then I asked her again why she was so unhappy.

"You would be too if you were me. I'm stuck in the house most of the time. I'll be happy when I get my driving license. That will mean freedom. I can't wait."

When she returned the next year she was still miserable with her life despite her car and driving license. This time she explained, "My parents are driving me crazy. I can't do anything. They have all these stupid rules. I even have to be home by 11pm on school nights. I can't be happy until I get out of the house and away from them and all their rules."

The next year she returned, still miserable. She had gone to her first year of college, boarding in a nearby state. Still a very unhappy young woman.

"School sucks. I don't have any money to do anything. When I graduate and get a job, then I will be happy."

I didn't say it to her but -- "Wanna bet?"

The result of my understanding and acceptance of my responsibility was astonishing. Most of the "reasons" for my unhappiness now showed themselves to be nothing but excuses. There was no longer a need to wait for anything in order to begin living happily. The thing to do was to begin working on being happy right now with what I had or I would remain in a misery of my own creation for the rest of my life.

How appropriate that my answer should have come on Independence Day.

So I began my Journey. I began using the tools that I had learned in my studies. The Eight common themes, the Eight Steps to Happier Living that I had learned from the great teachers of the past.

CHAPTER TWO

STEP TWO

ACCEPT WHAT YOU CANNOT CHANGE, ESPECIALLY OTHER PEOPLE

Everything in this universe can be divided into two categories; things we can change and things we can't.

When we try to control, we build a script in our minds and then fight reality when it dares to deviate from our script. Our lives will be more simple and happy when we stop trying to change the things that are beyond our control.

How exciting to awake each day with no preconceptions. To look forward to the unexpected without fear but with anticipation for the wonders the universe will reveal to us this day.

When we have practiced and worked on the achievement of acceptance we will be able to experience life with open willingness.

Some things that happen will be things we prefer. Some will be things we would prefer to do without. But each day will be filled with wonders.

Since imperfection is the human condition we all share, this imposes on us the duty to recognize that others can fall short of our expectations. This acceptance of the imperfection of others gives us the right to require that others accept ours.

Their unpredictable imperfection is what makes people exciting..

The urge to control the uncontrollable also allows us to neglect our main task -- - ourselves. That is where all our attention

16

should be concentrated. The job is big enough. It takes a lifetime to complete.

Acceptance is the key to happiness. Joyful, not grudging acceptance.

As we accomplish this, we will be able to live lives of confident spontaneity. Fear will be replaced by wonder and joy.

Question:

What in your life needs to be accepted to allow you to live more happily?

Sayings:

"Happiness is not about solving our problems. It is about living our problems."

MY JOURNEY TO STEP TWO

ACCEPT WHAT YOU CANNOT CHANGE, ESPECIALLY OTHER PEOPLE

The Journey to a happier life requires acceptance. It is also one of the most difficult Steps. Luckily for me two things happened that opened my eyes to the critical importance of this Step on my Journey.

Life teaches many lessons and those of us who have lived through a good deal of life have had many opportunities to learn. Opportunities usually occur when least expected. Some of us have taken advantage of these opportunities.

One such opportunity occurred when I was driving along the ocean in Boca Raton, Florida approaching a bridge over the Intracoastal Waterway. Another beautiful winter Florida day with temperature in the 70's, Mozart on the radio, and happiness in my soul. As I came up to the bridge, lights blinked, the bell clanged, the barriers dropped, and a huge, beautiful yacht approached the bridge. In those days the boats had the right of way so getting held up at the bridge was a common occurrence, particularly in winter.

As the boat passed there were some beautiful young women in bikinis on the foredeck waving and enjoying their situation immensely; the boat, the weather, their beauty, and the effect of it all, particularly them, on us gawkers.

I smiled and glanced at the man in the car next to me. He looked like a cartoon. I could almost see the smoke billowing from his ears, his curses turning the air blue. To emphasize his unhappiness he was pounding on his steering wheel doing nothing beneficial to either the wheel or his hands.

I had made a decision not to allow this delay that I couldn't change to take away my happiness. It was also clear that he had made a different choice.

John Doherty

(I told this story at a class on Happy Living that I gave recently. One of the participants in the class suggested another reason for the man's actions. "The other driver was so upset," he suggested, "because he was supposed to be on the boat.")

Studies have shown that those who attend religious services regularly are, on the whole, happier than those who don't. There are many benefits to organized religion besides the hope that God will smile upon you. Religion can provide a basis for the important and necessary skill of accepting those things we cannot change. It provides that solid community that we all desire and need. It leads us to nourish the spiritual side of our being. Religion is not the only place to find these benefits but it certainly serves up a large helping.

Years ago my pregnant religious daughter and her husband were visiting and she had a miscarriage, a spontaneous abortion. We rushed her bleeding and in pain to the nearest hospital where she learned that she had lost the baby. We were all devastated.

The next morning when she came to breakfast, gloom hung heavy over the table. My wife and I were incredibly upset. What had been planned as a happy vacation visit had turned into a disaster. Gina sat down and said she felt too sick to eat. None of us knew what to say.

Then Gina said, "Look. It happened. It is terribly unfortunate but there is nothing we can do about it. Besides, it's God's will."

She was able to accept with equanimity what I had considered a disaster. It was obviously one of those things that could not be changed. She was able to use "God's Will" as the tool that allowed her to accept it.

Whether you use a belief in God or some other way to accept what you cannot change doesn't matter. What matters is to decide whether or not the thing bothering you is something you can change. If it is something beyond your control, you have no choice but to accept it for no matter what you do, it will not change. The only thing that will be effective in terms of your happiness is to change your attitude toward it.

19

At first it was difficult for me to decide what was under my control and what was not. After struggling with things that didn't change despite my best efforts, I decided that there was a simple test. I tried to change whatever it was. If it changed, good. If it didn't, I classified it as one of those things beyond my control that I had to accept.

Letting go was easy for the small things, almost impossible for those I considered important or even necessary.

I was no better at accepting than most people when I began this Journey. So I started to practice. Epictetus advised. "Practice yourself on little things for heaven's sake, and then proceed to the greater." So I decided to practice on red lights. Still do.

When a red light has the audacity to hold me up on my "important" journey I call to mind that the light will hold me up at most for two or three minutes. Then I concentrate on living in the present, at least 'til the light changes. I look around and take in the sights, the sounds, the smells of where I am. I think about what I am doing. That I am overcoming my reluctance to accept things I cannot change. I try to relax and enjoy my mastery over myself. Sometimes I even succeed.

Did you ever notice that the length of time that a light remains red is directly proportional to the urgency of your need to get to your destination? Red lights are a gift of the universe. They are great two or three minute opportunities for learning patience, acceptance, and living in the present.

One of the most difficult things to accept is other people. They make mistakes we think are obvious. They ignore our sage advice to do things differently. They do things that hurt us and we cannot understand why they do them. They act selfishly and refuse to change their ways as we suggest.

One time my son Dan was visiting. We got in my car to go somewhere and he buckled up his seat belt.

For over 20 years I had stubbornly resisted the nagging of friends and loved ones to buckle up. For my own good, they said. I held firmly to my independence and refused. No argument or statistics could convince me to give up my right to do as I pleased. Even the laws some states passed were not enough to get me to change.

"Dan", I said. "Don't you trust your old man's driving?"

"It's not that, Dad" he replied. "But I work for an insurance company and I'm not stupid."

He didn't state the statistics that I had heard over and over. He didn't urge me to change my ways for my own good. He didn't tell me that I should buckle up because he loved me. He just stated two facts. He knew the odds and he was not stupid. Of course the inarguable fact was there. The fact that I could chose to continue to be stupid or I could change.

I changed and buckled up. I continued to buckle up after he left.

About a month later I was moving from my house in South Tamworth to my new home in North Sandwich, New Hampshire. About 2 miles from my new home was a small hill where the road took a sharp turn half way up the hill. The snow had begun about a half hour before I left my new house and drove back for another load of treasured possessions.

You guessed it. As I headed up the hill I slowed down but when I hit the turn the back of my pickup truck kicked out and I was soon climbing the hill sideways. Then the rear wheels found traction and shot me across the ditch and into the stone wall that bordered the road.

Up we went, taking off like Superman. The front of the truck rose into the air and I soon found myself in an upside down truck hanging suspended by my seat belt.

If I had not buckled up, I would have fallen on my head and most likely broken my neck.

Thank you, Dan!

Some time later I was telling the story to my friend, Randy. "Randy", I said. "I skidded out but I wasn't going very fast."

"Fast enough," Randy said.

When I look at my own life I realize that perhaps my judgments are not as good as I might like. Accepting that others have the right to make their own mistakes is difficult for all of us who think we are omniscient. But our lives will become much easier when we realize that almost everyone else thinks he or she is omniscient too.

I think the most difficult part of parenting is "Letting Go". It is necessary if our children are to learn, but the need to let go struggles with our desire to protect them. Balancing protection with the necessity of allowing them the benefit of growing through their own experience involves painful and difficult choices for any parent.

Acceptance is very difficult, especially the acceptance of the opinions, actions, and choices of others. We think that it is easy to see how others should act and think. But the evidence of our own lives should make it clear that our knowledge and advice is not really as good as we assume.

One time I was arguing with my wife Nancy about something, unimportant in retrospect, but of great import at the time. She had an opinion that I "knew" was obviously and unquestionably incorrect. Not only incorrect but dead wrong.

Carefully, I explained the errors in her thinking and outlined the reasons why her ideas were incorrect. She sat listening attentively. She wisely waited until I had finished. I concluded by saying confidently, "So, you see why I am right?'

"John", she said, "I know all that. I am aware of everything that you just said but I still don't agree with your conclusion."

I was stunned.

Incredible arrogance is at the root of our desire to control the world and the other people in it. Why do we dare to think that we know better than others what is best for them. Each of us has a hard enough time running our own lives without interfering in the lives of others.

Despite years of effort, the universe and others go on living and doing exactly what they want.

22

John Doherty

To accept the things we cannot change is the work of a lifetime. It gets easier with practice but never gets easy, especially with those things that we deem important.

Remember to practice on little things before you can expect to be able to overcome the big ones.

CHAPTER THREE

STEP THREE

LIVE IN THE PRESENT - ENTHUSIASTICALLY AND HONESTLY

All we ever have is this day, this hour, this moment. Only in the eternal NOW can we really experience and enjoy our lives. Yesterday is but a memory and tomorrow still a dream. Only in today can we do our living. Only by living today to the fullest and best of our ability can we improve our tomorrows.

The problems we must handle today are manageable. The ones we project for all our tomorrows will overwhelm us if we dwell on them. But they are not real. Most of our worries will never come to pass. Meanwhile, our lives will fly by unappreciated while we prepare for disasters that never strike.

All happiness dwells in today. Be alert and aware that real life is occurring now so you can seize the happiness it offers.

Eternity is today. Always with us. Here for the taking. Do not live in the world of dreams or regrets that exist only in your mind.

Reality is far is more exciting than anything our imagination can create. Only in today can we find the real rewards of living.

The eternal NOW. All experience, joy and sorrow within it.

Grasp it, live it, enjoy it.

Question:

Are there things in your life about which you can be enthusiastic?

John Doherty

Sayings:

"My life is full of disasters, most of which never occurred."

"Be present for your own life."

"Stop waiting and start living."

MY JOURNEY TO STEP THREE

LIVE IN THE PRESENT - ENTHUSIASTICALLY AND HONESTLY.

I have been fired from jobs. Not an enjoyable experience nor one I'd like to repeat but one that taught me a lot I really didn't want to learn. I had assumed that an outstanding person like myself was indispensable. I learned this was not the case and it wasn't easy to accept. Also, it soon became clear that the money I had saved would not last forever. Not even close.

Bills still came in. Expenses of living and job-seeking piled up. Savings shrank at an alarming rate. Fear and worry became my constant companions. My attitude, well, let's not mention it.

OK, I'll mention it. I'll never get a job! How will I pay the bills if I am not employed by the end of the month? Why did that jerk fire me? My happy life was now a rapidly fading memory.

Step One – I'm Responsible. Ha! I'm in control. Oh yeah? Those who won't give me a job are in control. The boss who fired me was in control. Finally, tiring of it all, I decided to see if the program I had developed could help. I reviewed my Eight Steps.

At Step Three, Live in the Present, I realized that this was the way out. The next day I started my new approach by working as hard as I could to find a new job until there was nothing left to do. I then took the rest of the day off. I refused to spend the rest of the day worrying about the future. I had the present.

Sometimes it came down to telling myself, "I have a place to live today, my health, enough food and clothes. Today, I'm OK."

With effort I was able to relax and at least to reduce my panic to simple concern. The day became enjoyable although I admit my worries continued to lurk on the horizon. I had to work hard to keep them out of each day. But my effort paid off even to the point where I could work on job hunting and then enjoy the rest of the day doing other things. It wasn't easy and I didn't always succeed. But I was able to turn my attitude around.

Dreams of the future that encourage us to work harder today to achieve them tomorrow are fine. Worries about what might happen are a waste of the precious present. We have so little time to enjoy life, to live and make a difference. How can we possibly waste any of it?

And I did get another job. …….. Eventually.

It seems so obvious that the present is all we have. We all know that the past is over and we cannot change it. We all know that worry will not change the future, only action will. Planning and action today have the power to change tomorrow. But we still worry, regret, and waste time that we could spend enjoying today. Why? As humans, it seems we are wired that way. Studies have shown that most of us spend up to 40% of our time thinking about the past or planning the future. We can retrain ourselves to live a better way.

We should remember that all the past we have is our memories. These "memories", no matter how realistic they seem, are far from a certain representation of what really happened. Cognitive Dissonance, the trick of our brain that alters our past memories to conform with what we wish had happened, makes our memory unreliable.

The future is not yet real. Only by working in the present can we affect it. So spending time in the past or the future is largely a waste for both are unreal. Only the present, the eternal present, is where we can truly live our lives.

It took a major event to finally propel me into enjoying my present life.

Back in 2006 I was diagnosed with Multiple Myeloma, an incurable form of cancer. I was told that my life expectancy was 3 to 5 years. Although at the time it did not seem to be the best news I had ever received, it was.

Death went from a theoretical reality to a certainty that could not be ignored. When death became real instead of theoretical I understood that my time to do all the things that I had put off was running out. So I started to do them and my life changed.

Each day of life became a gift. A gift to be lived to the fullest for I believed that I didn't have many days left. Living in the present was the only choice I had. The reality that my time was limited made living each day to the fullest not a difficult job but an easy and exciting one. Waking in the morning was a gift and each day an adventure.

Luckily, the diagnosis was incorrect. Nevertheless, it changed my life. I have Waldenstrom's Macroglobulanemia. It is not curable but, they told me, it was treatable. After a Clinical Trial that seemed to be working was cancelled, I went on the "Standard Treatment". Not only didn't it work but my condition got so bad that I thought that death was only a month or two away. I had no energy. Getting up in the morning was a chore beyond my ability. Life had become the simple process of waiting for death.

Then a new Clinical Trial was offered and it proved to be one of those miracles of modern medicine. Within a month my blood levels had retreated from transfusion range to simply low. Progress continued and I now have the energy that I had thought would be a memory.

Last Fall, my daughter Heather was visiting and we were celebrating my recovery. I live in the woods in New Hampshire and have a wonderful view of Whiteface Mountain. It had been one of my favorite hikes but I had not been able to hike it for over six years. "Why don't we give it a try?" asked Heather.

"I really don't think I can make it" I said.

"Let's just go as far as we can and if you can't go all the way we'll just come back."

Healthy, sensible Heather.

I made my usual hike preparations. PB&J sandwiches for the rest stop halfway up. No "hikers fare" for the top. I prepared and

28

John Doherty

packed Asparagus Vinaigrette, Tortellini Salad, Homemade Gingerbread. Of course, we made it to the top where we ate and luxuriated in the view and our accomplishment. Our silence spoke.

That night we celebrated with a three lobster dinner for each of us at Bayhaven, a restaurant in Cornish, Maine.

After my original death sentence I also stopped worrying about what others might think. It no longer mattered. I contacted my ex-wives and reconnected. After all, I once loved them deeply and I still cared. So I let them know. To my surprise and delight, in one case, my caring was reciprocated.

Once it became real to me that today was all I had, life became so important that I couldn't waste a single moment.

"Living in the Present" involves more than just "Paying Attention" or "Being Here Now". If this moment is all we have, then we better live it with enthusiasm and honesty. As Emily Dickinson said, "Life is so startling that it hardly leaves room for anything else!".

ENTHUSIASM

Before making happiness my primary goal, I used to drag through life, doing what I had to do, going where I was supposed to go, being who I thought I should be. My life was missing a key ingredient - enthusiasm.

When I began to live in the present I decided to stop living my life for other people. I now live it for myself and no longer care "what others might think". There is no time to waste with that. I thought I had little time left to live so I claimed it for myself.

I love to sing. I sing for myself so I sing a lot. William James said, "I don't sing because I'm happy. I'm happy because I sing." I don't know about that but sometimes I just feel like I have to burst into song. Luckily, most of these times I am alone. I don't sing for other people and used to be too embarrassed to let anyone hear me sing.

When I was visiting Nancy one winter she had been taking ukulele lessons and had become pretty good. As part of their graduation ceremony, each class member was supposed to get up on a small stage and perform.

When I was in high school I played the ukulele. I wasn't very good but had a good time with it. Nancy asked if I would join her and I gave my immediate habitual response to any request to perform in front of other people, "NO!"

She looked disappointed but resigned. I immediately realized that I was allowing the habits of a lifetime to rule me. I had always wanted to get up and sing but didn't because I was afraid of what others would think of me. But now I thought I was going to die soon so what did I care what others thought.

I agreed to accompany her and we practiced "Bill Bailey". I learned my simple part on the uke and the big night came, we both got up and strummed and sang. People clapped. We had a great time and we weren't bad. Not really good, but we weren't bad.

The freedom that the reality of my approaching death gave me infected my life like a virus. Joy at being alive today filled my life. Enthusiasm became a constant companion. I saw the wonder of everything, including me. So much to do and enjoy, so little time to accomplish it. Enthusiasm was almost overwhelming. The death sentence was a sentence to really live. At birth we are all sentenced to death but few are able to live with the acceptance of this reality.

HONESTY

Honesty is something we are told we should do because it is "good". Nonsense! Honesty is something to do because it gives us freedom. Freedom to be ourselves. No longer will we have to consider what others might think of our actions. We can relax and enjoy life being ourselves.

John Doherty

Integrity is something we talk about as being admirable and something for which we should strive, as if it were difficult to achieve. Well, it's not difficult. Integrity is just another way to say that a person is honest. Integrity comes from the Latin word meaning oneness. To me it means the freedom to relax and be myself.

I wish to be a man of integrity and to live as a whole person. Not wondering what others would think but doing what I think is best. It makes life so much easier. No longer do I have to try to remember the shadings and pretenses that I had used with different people in order to impress them. No longer do I have to remember the "white lies" and the excuses that would accompany my declining an invitation.

I used to think I was obliged to give reasons for my decisions. Often, this resulted in others providing solutions so I would do what they wanted me to do. If I said that I had to take my dog to the vet and couldn't go to the movies, they would say, "No problem. We'll pick you up at the vet's and we will have plenty of time to get there before the movie starts." Now, a simple "No thanks" suffices.

The freedom of honesty is an incalculable benefit. Since adopting it, my life has become easier and much happier. I have realized that "I don't feel like it" is an excuse with which no one can argue. I owe reasons for what I do only to myself.

So live each day with the freedom of honesty and the excitement of enthusiasm.

I now often meditate on death to keep it a reality in my life. I think about it so I will really live not just exist. So I will take chances. My time to do so is limited. So is yours!

CHAPTER FOUR

STEP FOUR

WANT WHAT YOU HAVE

Buddha said that unhappiness is caused by desire. We allow our wants or desires to become requirements for our happiness by calling them needs. We are the ones who determine these prerequisites.

Most of us spend our lives trying to get what we desire. We expend this tremendous effort in the belief that when we fulfill our desires we will be happy. This belief persists despite the evidence of a lifetime that all satisfaction is brief and ephemeral.

Each fulfilled desire is soon supplanted by a new one. That is the nature of the human animal.

We often confuse what we want with what we need. We can easily turn something that we want into something required for our happiness just by saying it is so. To be happier, work on getting rid of your desires, not satisfying them. Make sure that you have not convinced yourself that you need something that is just something you want. This simple shift in perspective is easier and far more effective than trying to satisfy your desires. We have little control over what we have. We can have complete control over what we want.

This does not mean giving up your dreams. Just make sure that your dreams remain preferences and are not promoted to requirements for your happiness.

The conditions we place on our happiness are self-imposed. We decide what we require to be happy. How simple to decide now to be happy with exactly what we have.

In order to get everything that you want, just want what you have.

Stop wanting and start enjoying. Enjoying what you have. Now.

Question:

Do you have any "needs" that are really disguised wants?

Sayings;

'What you have today is probably what you wanted yesterday."

"Don't work to have your life as you want it. Work to want it as you have it."

MY JOURNEY TO STEP FOUR
WANT WHAT YOU HAVE

Want to brighten up your day? Think of something you have that you really like. Now pretend that you don't have it any more. Really want it back, don't you? Now rejoice that you have it again. Feel better than when you started? How often possession blinds us to the thing we possess. Having things makes them ordinary. How different from when they were the objects of desire.

Buddha said that all unhappiness is caused by desire. Well I desire a lot of things and in many cases, unhappiness results when I don't get them or get them and then have them taken away.

In many cases, we do get what we want. We set a goal, work hard, and often achieve our goal. We are then rewarded with a feeling of success and the ability to enjoy what we have achieved. Then the happiness fades. So we set a new goal and repeat the process.

Meanwhile, most of the things we have are those we desired yesterday.   How much happier our lives would be if we concentrated on enjoying what we had rather than how to get what we want.

Most of the things in my life that bring me the greatest pleasure are those that I used to ignore or consider a job. Having friends in for a meal and conversation. Walking in the woods behind my house. Building a deck off my screen porch. Kayaking on a deserted pond with a lover. Having people to love and friends to share my life. My ability at 77 years of age to chop and split the firewood with which I heat my house.

The wonders of the world are breathtaking. I'm exploring spending two mornings a week making cutting boards. I'm planning hikes for this summer. I plan to finish this book and publish it in e-book form. I'm writing a book about ethics that has me excited. Hell, just living is exciting enough for a celebration so I'll have a big

John Doherty

"Potluck" for everyone I know as soon as the weather gets better and the bugs stop their feasting.

I have life. So do you. Not exactly as we would like? Tough! The life we have could be better but then it wouldn't be ours. I'm living and enjoying the one I have.

CHAPTER FIVE

STEP FIVE

CONTROL YOUR NEGATIVE EMOTIONS, PARTICULARLY ANGER

It is impossible to be happy while in the grip of a negative emotion. When these uninvited guests appear in your life, consider whether you will allow them to stay

Anger, jealousy, and revenge are some of the most common negative emotions that rob us of our happiness. The anger and revenge that we are told are acceptable are less than useless, they are dangerous.

There is no reason to allow them in our lives. We must make them leave if our happiness is not to be diminished.

The emotions are cunning. They will argue that they are "justified" or "righteous" and therefore have a right to remain.

Not true! You choose the guests you will invite into your home and you choose the emotions you will allow to reside in your soul.

Add to your life only the positive emotions that will increase your happiness. Banish the negative ones like anger and revenge that will diminish it no matter how they are disguised.

Common sense and self-interest dictate that the negative emotions should always be avoided.

Our emotions are the music that accompanies our lives. They are the spices that can turn our lives from vegetable stew into ratatouille

You can control your emotions. Make sure that you are the conductor of the symphony of your life.

36

John Doherty

Question:

What negative emotion would you be happier without?

Sayings:

"Allowing anger and unhappiness to stay in our lives is neurotic."

"We do things because of our thoughts and our emotions. To act in harmony with the universe, understand the first and control the second."

MY JOURNEY TO STEP FIVE

CONTROL YOUR NEGATIVE EMOTIONS, PARTICULARLY ANGER

The emotions are the music of your life. They are like the music that accompanies a movie and if you have ever seen a movie without music you know how much it enriches the experience. If it is too loud or does not fit the mood of the movie, it can ruin it.

Emotions are the same. Unless they are under control they can spoil the best experience. They help you appreciate the wonder of life and the wonder of other lives so different from your own. The beauty of nature, the excitement of a football game, the smile of your child or lover. The emotions can turn a life of vegetable stew into delicious ratatouille.

The emotions are like guests who show up at your home, sometimes uninvited. These guests then demand entry. They tell you that you must entertain them until they decide to go. Don't forget that it is your home. You are the one to decide who is to be welcomed as a guest and how long they will be welcome to stay.

The negative emotions sometimes arrive unbidden. The key factor is that you cannot be happy in the grip of a negative emotion. If you allow anger, jealousy, or any of the other negative emotions to reside in your soul, your happiness will suffer. Therefore, it is obvious that you should avoid harboring the negative emotions. For your own benefit. Why should you allow them to rob you of your happiness?

Often, a surge of emotion will surprise us. It is important to be aware that our response to this emotional surge is up to us. Many of the people I know seem convinced that their emotions are beyond their control. They seem to believe that unless these emotions are expressed they will cause great physical and mental harm. Venting, expressing, allowing the emotions to run their course is accepted as the proper way to handle them. Any other approach generates cries of "Don't suppress your emotions. It is dangerous to both physical and emotional health."

Research has shown that this is not true. It is a leftover from an old study of anger that has been shown to be fallacious. Anger allowed to express itself will generate not the relief that is sought but greater anger. Also, jealousy and other negative emotions will be increased by dwelling on them. Feeding these negative emotions will simply give them strength over you.

Always avoid the negative emotions for your own self-interest. This will improve your life. Sounds sensible but not at all easy.

The best approach to these unwanted visitors is to recognize what is happening. When in the grip of a negative emotion, immediately consider that it is robbing you of happiness and must be dealt with as soon as possible. Examine the emotion to discover its cause, the trigger that gave it birth. Then deal with the trigger. This will disarm the emotion that has taken control of you.

Anger is not "righteous" nor is revenge "justified". The Bible says, "Revenge is mine, saith the Lord." This wise advice urges us to leave revenge behind, to put it out of our lives for the sake of our own happiness. The same with anger, jealousy and all the other emotions that will rob you of your happiness.

According to Ralph Waldo Emerson, "For every minute you are angry, you lose 60 seconds of happiness". Not so dumb, old Ralph Waldo.

OK. So avoiding the negative emotions is a good idea. "But how do I control my anger? I find it extremely difficult." I hear you say. Remember that to control anger or any of the other negative emotions first recognize that they are under your control. Anger or one of the others may show up suddenly in your life but it is up to you whether you allow it to remain.

The emotions bubble up through the limbic system in response to triggers. Adrenalin and other chemicals are secreted into the bloodstream. But the limbic system does not analyze. It responds –

to triggers. These emotions conjured up by your limbic system can be brought under control by your analyzing prefrontal cortex, the more recent evolutionary development of your brain. As the body responds to the chemical changes, the prefrontal cortex does its job, analyzes the changes in the body and seeks to determine what caused the surge. The analysis of the trigger that caused the emotion is often simply a justification for the emotion we feel. The justification may be correct or it may be an excuse. But often we realize that the emotion is not justified. It is up to us to analyze the cause and then take steps to deal with it.

This concentration on the trigger and away from the emotion itself will take strength from the emotion and put strength where it is more useful, correcting or encouraging the cause.

If it is a positive emotion that increases our happiness it should be encouraged. If it is negative and reducing our happiness we should try to reduce it. This is best accomplished by dealing with the trigger. This will remove our attention from the emotion itself and direct it to the action we must take.

Advice on controlling the negative emotions has been provided by sages for thousands of years. Provided and ignored. The latest research shows that the best way to control the negative emotions is to put the emotion off while you deal with the cause. Horace said in the first century BC, "When angry, count to 10." Mark Twain said, "When very angry, count to 100." If we allow the negative emotions free rein, if we "experience" them fully, they will simply grow. Ignore the emotion and deal with its cause and they will wither.

Epictetus said, "If you would cure anger, do not feed it. Say to yourself: 'I used to be angry every day; then every other day; now only every third or fourth day.' When you reach thirty days offer a sacrifice of thanksgiving to the gods." This is advice worth listening to even 2000 years later. Modern science agrees.

I used to have an anger problem. I allowed anger to spoil many a perfect day. I had been studying happiness for a few years and intellectually, I knew that I should banish anger from my life. But it seemed an impossible task

There is a great difference between "believing" something to be true and really knowing it in your gut. That realization, the "gut knowledge" about anger came for me one beautiful winter day when I lived in Florida. As usual the temperature was in the low seventies and the sun was shining in a blue sky dotted with puffy white clouds. My car radio was playing beautiful music as I drove along Deerfield Beach Boulevard. My soul was peaceful and happy as I enjoyed the beautiful day. Life was sweet.

Then I saw that traffic up ahead had slowed to a crawl. Road construction forced two lanes of traffic to merge into one. No worries mate! I realized that the delay would be brief. As we inched forward past the sign that said, "Alternate", I happened to glance at the car next to me. The driver glanced back, then stared a challenge. I knew he would try to push in front of me, ignoring the sign, ignoring the rules of fair play built into every human being.

How dare he! We'll see who chickens out! I was a New Yorker and there was no way this yokel was going to push in from of me! I had been brought up and survived with some of the pushiest people on the planet. OK buddy, just try it!!

He tried and, to my embarrassment, the one who "chickened out" was me. I gave way. I let him push in front of me. Shame, embarrassment, then rage at him and even more at myself for showing up my weakness.

The next thing I knew I was roaring down the Boulevard at 65 miles an hour chasing this guy. I wanted to catch him, pull him over to the side of the road and beat him to a pulp. I won't argue that my feelings were inappropriate, childish, and foolish but they were my feelings.

As I raced after him sanity returned. I pulled over to the side of the road, heart racing as I panted for breath. I realized that 5 minutes earlier I had been at peace with the world, and my life had been happy. Now unhappy and controlled by my rage, I was allowing this situation, this guy, to replace that happiness.

As I sat there regaining my composure I realized that I was the guy who had taken away my happiness by giving in to my rage. I also realized that I had no idea why he had pushed in front of me. Maybe he had been fired and was extremely upset. Maybe he was rushing to the hospital because someone he loved had been in an accident. Maybe his wife had gone into labor and he was rushing to take her to the hospital. Maybe he didn't realize that he was going out of turn. Or, most likely, he was just an asshole.

The point was that I was allowing him to rob me of my happiness. I decided that I would refuse to allow that to happen.

Speaking of assholes, that reminds me of a story.

A group in which I participated was talking about "Road Rage". Most agreed that it was a frequent problem since so many people nowadays were extremely impolite and nasty. Many had examples of the species that they had met while driving. There were plenty of stories to demonstrate how difficult driving had become.

Louise raised her hand. She was older, retired, and extremely proper. She wore white gloves and had a hat on her blue tinged hair. Louise spoke like an English teacher because that is what she had been and would always be.

"Well" Louise said, "I used to have a problem with "Road Rage" but I don't any longer. Every time I leave to go out to drive somewhere I always tell myself that before I get where I am going I am going to meet an asshole."

We were shocked at her uncharacteristic choice of words and she smiled pleasantly at her ability to shock us.

"Then", she continued, "when someone cuts me off or pushes into the parking place for which I was heading, I say to myself "there you are you asshole. I knew I would meet you today and there you are". Then I go about my business."

I don't know if it was the word "asshole" coming from this genteel lady's mouth or the wisdom of what she had to say but I never forgot her or her secret. Even now, 25 years later, when some other driver acts like a jerk, I just smile and think of Louise.

John Doherty

Recently I was going out to dinner with my friend Ralph, his wife Marilyn, and our friend Wanda. As we were leaving, Ralph got on the subject of bad drivers and how furious it made him. Marilyn joined in and said that driving with him had become uncomfortable since he usually got really angry before they arrived.

So I told them the story of Louise and the assholes.

Sure enough, we had gone only 10 miles or so and some idiot coming the other way was driving in the middle of the road and forced us into the verge. Ralph exploded.

Marilyn said, "There you are. I knew we were going to meet you today."

Marilyn, Wanda and I exploded with laughter. After a simmering pause, Ralph joined in.

You are responsible for your happiness. Despite what you are told, you can control your emotions. "I was angry, jealous, fearful etc." is no excuse for poor behavior or for surrendering even one moment of your life that could be happier.

CHAPTER SIX

STEP SIX

PARTICIPATE IN A GROUP

THAT WILL PROVIDE THE BENEFITS OF COMMUNITY.

We humans are social animals. Just as we view the miser as an unhealthy human being, so too, the hermit is perceived as an oddity.

The company of our fellows confirms that we are not alone in this difficult journey from birth to death. This journey to the unknown during which we lack control over much of what happens to us.

We humans gather in cities and towns, not only for protection but also for the simple pleasure of being with our fellows. Of seeing that we are not the only ludicrous animal. That there are others just as laughable.

We need to communicate and share with others. We need to give as well as receive. We get comfort and strength from this joining and interaction. Sharing can increase our joy and make our pain more tolerable. It can make the intolerable, tolerable and the happy, joyful.

The basis of all religion is community and wonder; the knowledge that we are part of something greater than ourselves. Something with meaning and purpose in which we play our part, even if we do not know what that part may be.

Join some group. Almost any group. Meet others who share your interests or explore new ideas. Your life will be enriched and your happiness will increase.

John Doherty

Question:

Is there a group you want to make time to join?

Sayings:

"Sharing lightens sorrow and increases joy."

"Joy is doubled when it is shared. Sorrow is cut in half,"

MY JOURNEY TO STEP SIX

PARTICIPATE IN A GROUP THAT WILL PROVIDE THE BENEFITS OF COMMUNITY.

From the time we are small we are urged to be independent. We praise our children for it. We admire it when we think we see it in others. We all long to be self-sufficient. Independence is held up as a goal to be prized. We even have a holiday to celebrate it.

Silliness! It's an illusion! None of us is independent. Not a single one of us.

Humans are social animals. We are completely dependent on others. On the society in which we live. From others we learn to speak. To read. To pray. To live. Without others we would not have food, clean water, safety. We need others for wisdom. For our existence.

We need others so that we might give as well as receive. We have a built in need not only to seek knowledge but to teach, to share our knowledge as well as our excess possessions. Others help us realize that we are not alone in this difficult journey of life. Others have shown the way, not only how to live but how to die. We need others.

We need to share this exploration of living, this struggle to discover the meaning or even if there is a meaning in our lives. The sharing of life with its joys and sorrows, learning and mistakes, provides meaning in our lives. Lives that might otherwise be empty and without purpose.

Isaac Newton said that he "stood on the shoulders of giants". We, too, owe much to the explorers who have gone before us into new lands, physical, intellectual, and spiritual. Lao Tse, Buddha, Jesus Christ, Socrates, Aristotle, Newton, Einstein, are but a few to whom we owe so much.

John Doherty

The wheel, domesticated animals, cooking, writing, the concepts of morality and spirituality were all given to us by nameless heroes, both male and female.

Just as the miser is considered one who does not know the true value of money, so the hermit is one who makes himself a pauper by rejecting the richness of living that community provides.

I see articles and hear people bemoan modern society and the lack of physical interaction in the lives of the younger generation. Communication through e-mail, texting, Facebook, and Twitter are demonized as causing separation from "real" communication.

It was ever thus. When books came about, the loss of the personal in the exchange of ideas and stories was bemoaned. We are poorer, said the old ones. Then literacy spread widely and letters replaced visiting and talking. Oh dear, they moaned. Then the telephone. Oh, you don't even see the person face to face. It's so impersonal.

Then radio, TV, and now the Internet. "Here we go again" as they moan about losing the personal side of interaction, of building a community. It's now so mechanical and impersonal they say.

No method of communication is perfect. Even words are poor substitutes for reality. Each method should be taken for what it is. It should be gloried for its advantages. The reality of what it cannot achieve accepted.

Communities have many structures, none perfect. Family, nation, town, friends, clubs, and even friends on Facebook. Some of these social structures are very different from the ones to which we are accustomed. Some communities are based on sharing to the extent that they have not even invented money. Others have based lives on a commonly held belief in a God. But no perfect community has arisen yet.

We must work with what we have. Admit the bad and utilize the good.

Modern methods of communication substitute reach, numbers, and immediacy for close and more personal methods of communicating. The reach of the internet is astounding. Distance and the vast numbers of people that can be reached make us older ones gasp. The young take it as natural to their world.

My granddaughter decided to teach herself Mandarin Chinese. She got on the Internet and did so over the summer. That autumn when she got to her first year of college she enrolled in a course in Mandarin. The teacher asked her if she came from a Taiwanese family because she had a Taiwanese accent. She had picked it up in a chat room with Chinese people who happened to live in Taiwan. She lives in Savannah Georgia!

This is the new community. Not the one I grew up with, but a far better one. The old ways may not be used as often, some have been largely replaced with new methods, but they are still available and utilized for those intimate moments of sharing that goes beyond mere words.

I was visiting Nancy in North Carolina this winter and decided to cook a special meal. Then I realized that all my cookbooks were at home and the special vegetarian recipe that I had planned was not available.

"Use the Internet," she said. Duh! I Googled the recipe and found thousands of variations as well as the original. At my fingertips. I had joined a larger community than I ever suspected was out there.

Community will add to the happiness in our lives if we work at it. A community is not something that you just belong to. You have to want to be part of it, recognize your part in it, and then work at it. You have to recognize what you have to offer, what value you can add. This includes both giving and taking.

Even a group of fledgling poets needs someone with expertise to teach them the basics but they also need an audience to listen and provide feedback both positive and negative.

In my journey, my awakening to the importance of community came back in 1974 when I realized that I was using alcohol as my prescription for facing the problems and pain in my life. That prescription was not effective for more than short periods and left more problems in its wake than it solved.

John Doherty

I joined a 12 step group and listened. After a month or so I decided that what I heard made sense and I stopped drinking. The community of the group became, for a time, my whole world. Telephone, coffee, meetings took up most of the time when I wasn't working. My life changed.

Through my new community I acquired new friends as well as an entirely new set of living skills that had been unknown to me. I saw how others were facing the same problems that were beyond my coping skills and doing it well. Their lives may have been difficult but they were under control and reasonable.

My new community offered me encouragement, wisdom, and support. They saved my life and set me on the path to honing the skills I had learned about how to cope with life.

How wonderful it is to belong to a community with others who share your enthusiasm. For stamps. For giving to others. For sharing a religious belief. Or a political one. For reading. For tennis. You are able, particularly through the Internet, to find a community designed for any interest you might have.

How much that community can enrich your life! It allows you to give as well as receive and both increase happiness. It allows you to teach and to learn. It enriches your understanding that we are all so similar, doing our best to be happy and get along. It helps us to realize that the world described in the headlines is not the real world in which we live. We live in a world of real people, mostly like us, waiting to be our friends or acquaintances.

Our social needs are bred into our genes. The social aspect of our lives has been determined by evolution and is one of the reasons that we have prospered as a species. Many studies have proved beyond doubt that cooperation is a far more effective survival strategy than any other and that competition is not one that holds any long term promise.

As you increase the quality of your participation in communities you can deepen your appreciation of others. By accepting the riches they offer you can increase the happiness in your life.

CHAPTER SEVEN

STEP SEVEN
MEDITATE. IT FEEDS YOUR SPIRIT

We would not dream of going a day or a week without feeding our bodies. Without food, our appetite demands satisfaction.

But our soul is quiet. When we neglect to provide it with the sustenance it needs, it does not scream for attention. It just withers slowly.

Our lives are busy. Busy with the demands of earning a living, coping with situations, and interacting with the others in our lives. We are so busy that we often neglect to take the brief time necessary to feed our souls.

Our soul needs to consider the reason for our being, lest we forget. It needs to become aware of the beauty and wonder of the world around us, lest we forget. It needs to contemplate the excitement and individuality of others, lest we become self-centered. It needs to listen to nature and to music, to see the clouds, the waves, the stars, lest our downcast eyes see only the dirt and muck and forget that this is where life was born.

Meditation - thinking about being, beauty, love, wonder, kindness, happiness, acceptance, and the oneness of all – is the necessary food of the soul. With meditation, our soul will bloom like a plant that is fertilized and watered. We will produce in our lives all those wonderful things we contemplate in our meditation.

Question:

Can you picture a dream and float with it, enjoying it without promoting it to a need?

50

John Doherty

Sayings:

"If meditation is a chore, you're not doing it right."

MY JOURNEY TO STEP SEVEN
MEDITATE. IT FEEDS YOUR SPIRIT

A long, long time ago, when I was young, I was very religious and captured by the idea of God. To my father's disgust and frustration, I decided to give up a college scholarship and become a Trappist monk. I wanted to spend the rest of my life in meditation and contemplation of God. I did go to the monastery although I didn't stay for long. The experience was one that has had a great and positive influence on the rest of my life.

I have never lost the knowledge of how important the things we call "spiritual" are to a healthy existence. But I also found that these things we call "spiritual" are not something separate from our everyday lives. Instead of thinking of the "spiritual" as occupying some separate sphere of existence, a higher realm, I found that "spiritual" is just another aspect of our human existence.

Meditation is not something "nice" but something necessary for the spiritual side of us.

In his book, "10% HAPPIER" Dan Harris talks about his interview with the Dalai Lama. He challenges the Dalai Lama's statement that our unhappiness comes from self-centeredness. "Don't we need to be somewhat self-centered in order to succeed in life?" he asked.

"Self–centeredness is natural," the Dalai Lama responded. "But the practice of compassion, concern for the well-being of others, that is of immense benefit to oneself. ... So I usually describe: we are selfish but be wise selfish rather than foolish selfish."

If meditation is not fun, enjoyable, interesting, easy, relaxing, and exciting, you are not doing it right.

It is not the boring, difficult practice that so many teach and preach. Without getting all dewy-eyed about it, real meditation is connecting with that side of ourselves that we call "spiritual".

John Doherty

Do you remember when you were very young and lay in the grass looking up at the clouds drifting by? Do you remember thinking of nothing as you lay there, your mind drifting as you were caught up in a world beyond the one that you inhabited most of the time? Meditation.

Meditation is something widely recommended but little practiced. Few do it because most of the instructions seem difficult if not impossible. Those who follow the instructions they are given soon get bored or find the steps they are told to take beyond their ability. They quickly lose interest and that is a shame.

There are many types of relaxing the mind that are taught as techniques of meditation. Many of them are beneficial. But these are not what I am encouraging. What I urge is getting in touch with that part of the existence of each of us that is beyond the ability of words to express. The side of life that we crave that is beyond the material world we grasp so easily. Yet it is an integral part of our world. Beauty, love, kindness. Integral parts of living yet somehow different from it. This is the realm that our spirit urges us to explore.

Meditation is something we all do. Every time you recall a fond memory, a place you love, a song that makes your heart leap, a person who can make you smile, the love you see in a child, the physical beauty in a person; these are meditations. Thinking about kindness, love, friendship, or excellence in any endeavor is also meditation.

No particular position is required You can do thinking anytime, anywhere. We all do.

Before we get into what meditation is and how to do it, let's look at what it's not. It is not sitting in a particular position. It is not emptying the mind or repeating a set of words or sounds. These things may be nice but are not necessary.

The meditation that I recommend is getting in touch with the spiritual side of our being, the part of us that is quiet. Art, beauty, music, dance, nature, kindness, love, excellence; these are the things and the thoughts that we should never abandon if we wish to live completely.

In both the western and eastern traditions there are two types of meditation. Most of the discussion you hear about meditation is about what is known as "Contemplation" in the west or "Transcendental Meditation" in the east. This is wonderful and provides many spiritual and physical benefits but is a terrible place to start because it takes lots of practice to do it well and easily.

Start with simple meditation. It, too, provides many spiritual and physical benefits and is easier to learn. This type of meditation is just thinking

The word "meditate" comes from the Latin word "meditatio" which means to think. So in the beginning forget all that nonsense about emptying your mind. Thinking is easy. Emptying your mind is almost impossible. Meditation is just thinking about wonderful things. Things that lift up that part of you that we call spirit. Things that lift you out of yourself. A favorite song. A wonderful basket by Michael Jordan that you can play over and over in your mind. A movie that moved you. A person you love. A scene that brings you peace.

Another path is to think of someone or something for which you are grateful. Consider that gratitude, how you would express it to another person or the universe at large or whatever you might think of as "God". Get one of these things and keep it in your mind for 60 seconds, just one minute. You have just meditated.

The second type of meditating is called Contemplation or Transcendental Meditation. This is a union of yourself with the universe or what many call God. It isn't easy. But much of the instruction given is unhelpful.

When you have arrived at the state where you enjoy thinking meditation and you have gone beyond the minute you used when you began, try this. Many tell you to empty your mind. Can't be done. Don't waste your time trying. Let your mind fill with whatever it wants.

54

John Doherty

Then think of the unthinkable. The unimaginable. Eternity. Infinity. The concept of a God. The size of the universe. Or the number of dollars in our national debt. If you let your mind drift to infinity, the wonder of the universe, those wonders that cannot be understood or explained, then your mind will stand in silent wonder and be filled.

Let yourself become part of timeless immensity. These impossible thoughts will drive out any minor considerations that your mind insists on. The clutter will disappear to be replaced by the unknowable all.

The Bible says in Psalm 48, "Be still, and know that I am God."

Be still.

Be still. How difficult. Our minds refuse. The chatter in my head goes on like the wings of a butterfly. Like the buzzing of a bee, thoughts ceaselessly and carelessly skim across my consciousness. As if they had importance when stillness and wonder are what's really important.

It is easiest to float off into this universal connection when gazing into a fire, lying on your back looking up at the stars, or sitting on the beach watching the waves roll in. Sitting quietly with your eyes closed is also effective. But after doing it for a while you will find it attracts you and becomes easier. I do it when driving long distances in the car. Sometimes shorter ones. I steal moments to make that connection with whatever is. The great thing of which I am a part.

Let the spiritual part of yourself wordlessly enjoy this state. Afterward, don't analyze it. Just remember how good and peaceful and complete it felt.

A Poem by John Doherty

Who could have dreamed a flower
The sea, a star, the sky
If given all eternity
I guarantee, not I.

John Doherty

CHAPTER EIGHT

STEP EIGHT
PRACTICE, PRACTICE, PRACTICE

Competence is the reward of practice. The more you practice, the better you will get.

Living happily is like knitting or driving a car; if you practice these Eight Steps, you will become more proficient, more competent, and happier.

Do not fear "failure". It is part of the learning process. As you try, you will learn. As you learn, the skills will become second nature.

Remember to practice on small things. Life will provide you with enough that are really difficult.

Most of our lives are little things. If we can succeed in living the little situations happily, most of our lives will be happy. Who knows? You may get so proficient that you will be able to live happily through the big things, too.

LEARNING + PRACTICE = HAPPINESS

Questions:

Are you willing to put in the effort required to make your life happier? Is there one of the Steps that seems most appropriate for you to practice right now?

Sayings of Epictetus:

"No great thing is created suddenly, any more than a bunch of grapes or a fig. If you tell me that you desire a fig, I answer that there must be time. Let it first blossom, then bear fruit, then ripen."

"Practice yourself, for heaven's sake, in little things; and from them proceed to greater."

John Doherty

MY JOURNEY TO STEP EIGHT
PRACTICE, PRACTICE, PRACTICE

And now we get to the hard part. Practice, the thing they tell us "makes perfect". If not perfect, at least a heck of a lot better.

The opportunities for practice are constant. It is the awareness of them that is difficult. The ability to realize that every time you are not feeling happy that it is up to you to do something about it.

We know what to do and how to do it. But making the effort, the almost constant effort that is required to cultivate this awareness is hard. It is so easy to be distracted by the immediacy of living: the problems and the minor pleasures that so easily take our concentration from the main job, living happily.

No one thinks that he or she can want to be a good tennis player, want it really badly, then walk out on the court at Wimbledon and win. Who would expect to join the New York Yankees and be a .400 hitter without years of effort? Skills are developed through learning and practice. Living happily is a skill and must be learned and practiced like any other skill.

The skills required to live happily have been preached for centuries by wise men. Some of these skills are outlined in this book. The practice is up to you.

Aristotle said happiness is a life lived according to virtue. Others say it is a life that has meaning. Each of us, as the Dalai Lama says, must answer this question for him or herself. It requires not only an examination of the living skills we have developed but also of how we relate to our fellow human travelers.

This book gives a guide from the wisdom of the ages about how to live one's life more happily. The tools it provides will ensure that your life will be a happier one if you employ them. But "What makes true happiness" is a question that only you can answer for yourself.

Meanwhile, the tools to live a happier life are in the Eight Steps. Practice is the hardest step.

I know many unhappy people who complain that life is a misery. Their lives would be happy if only they had…. If only others did….if only …if only.

I ask if they practice trying to be happy. They look at me like I am crazy. They don't understand why happiness doesn't just happen. They wait, hoping and expectant, for happiness to fall upon them as a gift from heaven. Occasionally, it does but only in brief dribs and drabs that serve to whet the appetite and ensure a craving for more. The hedonic happiness we will discuss in the next section is what they hope for. They hope it will return and complain if it doesn't. But they do little to make real happiness happen.

No one expects to learn to drive a car without learning how the pedals work and then practicing driving, hopefully in a large deserted parking lot. No one expects to know how to read without learning their ABC's and then practicing. Why should living happily be any different?

A great chess player, a great musician, a wonderful painter, a skilled athlete, all have worked hard to learn the basics of their craft and then to practice. No matter how blessed with natural ability, it will come to naught without practice.

Practice is often boring. It requires repetition and takes time from other pleasures. But it is necessary.

Practicing the skill of happier living is an easier thing to practice than most. The skill is for living, something that we do constantly so the opportunity to practice is always present. It just requires attention to what is important, to the goal of life; happiness. The only goal, Aristotle says, that we seek for its own sake.

We watch a child learning to walk, a most difficult skill. First the child watches others walk around, speedily getting to the things the child wants to reach. After watching, the child tries. He pulls himself up then steps out …. and falls down.

Again and again he tries and fails. But the child does not consider it failure, he thinks of it as "learning to walk". Finally, after weeks of practice and effort, he takes a step. Then another. Then he walks! Get out of the way!

So, if you really wish to live more happily, you have to work for it. As Benjamin Franklin said, "The harder I work, the luckier I get." So the more you practice these Steps, the happier you will make your life.

Living the Eight Steps

It is a human failing that we wish to allocate blame elsewhere when we make a mistake.

Once, in the darkness of a winter night, my wife and I went out to dinner in New York. Luckily I found a parking place on the slush covered icy street. As I got out the driver's side of the car, my wife exited the passenger side and, as she stepped to the sidewalk, she slipped on the ice and went down into the slush, good dress and all.

Trembling with frustration, tears in her eyes, she looked up at me. "You pushed me!"

We laughed later but the urge to place blame elsewhere is almost irresistible.

Accept the responsibility for your life. Once you do, you will also have taken control. Your life is called yours because it is you who controls much of what happens but most importantly how you react to it. (Step One)

Practice accepting the things you cannot change, the little things. We get so many opportunities to do this. It is wonderful practice for the few big disappointments that will inevitably come our way. Using the little annoyances as practice will prepare us to handle the inevitable big problems better if not perfectly. (Step Two)

Take time during a day you consider "busy" and make sure you are alive. Don't let your life escape you by living it in the past or the future. Make it a practice to recall yourself into the present frequently as you go about your day. You will be surprised at what you find. (Step Three)

Enjoy what you have. When working to achieve something or to acquire some object look at what you have and remember to enjoy it. It is probably what you spent time in the past trying to get. (Step Four)

When a negative emotion invades your life and attacks your happiness, fight it. Always. For your own sake. Make your happiness your priority and don't allow the negative emotions that so frequently bubble up at the unfairness of life to diminish it. (Step Five)

Be aware of the communities to which you belong. Loved ones, friends, neighbors, those with whom you share a goal or an interest. Reach out and accept the happiness that these contacts provide and search out new ones. (Step Six)

Look up. Tear your gaze from the grit and labor of life and look up to the stars. Life, creation, is a wonderful thing. Make sure that you allow yourself the time and make the effort to enjoy the world outside yourself. Consider the beauty, the complexity of creation and your part in it. (Step Seven)

Practice by doing these things constantly. Make the priority in your life, not achieving, getting, or accumulating, but living. Living happily. You can achieve it by utilizing the tools I have outlined but only if you practice them. Often. Eventually, with practice, they will become habits and determine how happy your life is. (Step Eight)

When you are having a bad day, look to the Eight Steps and see which one would make you happier if you practiced it immediately.

The practice of happier living is a constant awareness that true happiness is the goal of life. All else is frivolity. Realize that seeking to live happily is not a selfish task. It is focused not only on ourselves but also on our relation to the rest of humanity.

Live happily! It's up to you.

John Doherty

HAPPINESS

WHY IS HAPPINESS SUCH A NEGLECTED SUBJECT?

Everyone wants to be happy, don't they?

Why do so many spend their whole lives seeking to earn more money, to get a promotion, to be admired, to acquire "stuff", to lose weight? Why do so many concentrate so hard on so many secondary goals they think will make them happy and ignore the main goal, happiness itself?

If happiness is so important, why isn't it taught in schools? Our schools teach many things, but not how to be happy. We award prizes for reading, writing and arithmetic, but not for learning how to live happily. We have schools of agriculture, science, law, medicine, but no schools of happy living.

Why not?

One reason is that we humans want to achieve. In his book "Drive" Daniel Pink points out that we work at our maximum level not because of rewards and punishments but because we enjoy progressing, succeeding in accomplishing tasks, getting proficient at a skill.

Financial success is easy to measure and display. Happiness, not so much. Even the plethora of psychological studies that began in the late twentieth century admit that this is something that is self-measured. So we foolishly spend time and effort to be the first among our peers to get the newest toy, the biggest house, the most prestigious job. We substitute these false goals for the real goal of living, true happiness.

True happiness is such an elusive goal that we can't even measure our own progress. Are we happier today than yesterday? Are we coping better with the problems of living now than we did last week? How can we tell? The problems we faced last week or yesterday are different from the ones we face today. Our circumstances are different. We all like to measure progress. To measure our progress in living happily is extremely difficult.

I used to jog 5 miles every day and enjoyed getting out by myself and running until I was sweating and "hit my stride". The "Runner's High" that came after the first ten minutes or so made my exercise effortless and enjoyable.

Best of all I loved to see my progress. Today I ran farther than yesterday or ran the 5 miles 2 seconds faster than last week. Today I was able to run up the big hill without slackening my pace. These were the treasured rewards by which I measured my success.

Without progress, running would have been simply exercise to maintain my health. It would have been a job, not an enjoyable hour of effort.

It is easy to measure accomplishment in the things we work at so hard, those things that take up so much of our time and effort. We diligently slave away at a job we dislike to earn more money, to get a promotion. We diet and exercise to get thinner, to improve our health. How much time do we spend each day at trying to learn how to be happier?

The second reason for the lack of attention in our schools to the skills of living happily is that there are three professions that claim it as their exclusive area of study and proficiency. Religion, psychiatry, and philosophy all claim to be the guardians of the knowledge of how to live happily. Each will battle fiercely if one of the others claims to have answers that exclude their approach.

This claim to exclusive rights to the subject prevents the widespread and cooperative study that is necessary for progress. The squabbling and jealousy prevents each from benefitting from discoveries of the others and prevents the spread of that knowledge through education.

The Dalai Lama was asked, "What would you do if science disproved one of your beliefs?" He replied, "Why, I would change my beliefs." Not a common outlook.

John Doherty

Two very interesting studies reveal much about how we measure. The first was a study of paraplegics and their emotional health after therapy. After a devastating accident that resulted in loss of the use of arms or legs, life was certainly different. At first, probably a disaster. But after one year it was found that the distribution of happiness among the population studied was almost the same as for the general population. These people had adapted to their new life and their outlook was generally the same as for the rest of us.

The other study of those whose lives had changed completely was of lottery winners. Just as for the paraplegics, the happiness distribution one year after winning the big bucks, the lottery winners were in the same boat as the rest of us. The happy ones were still happy, the ones who had been unhappy before winning were still unhappy a year later.

What the heck does it all mean? The research revealed two surprising answers.

The first answer was that we tend to judge our current circumstances against our recent past not against our former hopes. The recent past was found to be somewhere between six and nine months.

The same for both the good and bad. Lottery winners and paraplegics. For the lottery winners, the big win that was supposed to change their lives and make them happy was now judged not against their former income but against the previous six months or so when they were already wealthy. The paraplegics could look back over six or nine months of progress in coping with their disability.

The second answer from these studies is that we tend to compare with our peers. The paraplegics were comparing their lives with other paraplegics. Those in rehab had the ability to compare with those just beginning and the skills they had learned made them far better able to cope than more recent arrivals. After time went by the lottery winners were comparing with other rich people.

This is also why bereavement groups help us cope with our loss.

Bereavement is subject to the same rules of time and comparison with others in similar circumstances. It is said that "Time heals all wounds". It may not heal them completely but it does make them tolerable. The death of a loved one is terrible and tragic but the pain and loss does fade with time. In the initial shock, the idea that time will help seems like betrayal of the loved one who has been lost. But life will work its own ways and time will certainly help.

Being with others who have also suffered great loss will help, too. The human ability to empathize, to realize that we are not alone in our sorrow helps. The magic of community not only increases our joys but makes our sufferings more tolerable.

John Stuart Mill was a brilliant man but he was wrong when he said "If you seek happiness you will never find it." This depressing "truism" has been accepted by too many for too long. It makes as much sense as saying "If you want to learn to drive a car, driving lessons will not help." Or, "If you want to learn to cook, don't read cookbooks."

Living happily is a skill just as driving a car, cooking, reading, or playing tennis are skills. First you learn the basic rules and then you practice what you have learned. The more you practice, the better you will get.

Perhaps you will never be the best at cooking or tennis but you will be a lot better than you were before you learned and practiced. The same with living happily. There are skills to learn that will help. Practice may not make perfect but it certainly makes better.

WHAT IS HAPPINESS?

It's easy to say we want to be happy but very difficult to say exactly what that is.

As Supreme Court Justice Potter Stewart said of pornography, "I can't define it but I know it when I see it." We can say the same about happiness. Defining happiness has occupied philosophers

John Doherty

and other thinkers for centuries and no common definition has been accepted yet.

Aristotle defined happiness as "A life lived according to virtue. The only goal we seek for its own sake. The whole aim and end of human existence." When Aristotle used the word "virtue" he did not mean "Be Good" as we were so often told when we were young. Virtue to Aristotle meant those ways of acting that are effective. Effective ways of living that resulted in happy lives.

He advised living a life of moderation. For example, he talked of the virtue of courage that is only a virtue when used in moderation. Too much and one becomes foolhardy. Too little and the result is cowardice.

Psychiatry generally holds happiness as the ultimate goal to be sought through self-actualization; achieving the best that we can be.

The religion in which I was raised taught that the purpose of life was "To know, love, and serve God in this world and be HAPPY with Him forever in heaven".

We can make statements about what happiness is not and this is helpful. One false goal that occupies many is the desire for "Hedonic Happiness". That is the feeling that results when you get something that you want like a new car or when something that you desire happens to you. Say the object of your dreams agrees to go on a date or you win the Lottery. "Hedonic" happiness is generally caused by something outside ourselves. Obviously happiness is not just satisfying every desire that pops up.

The major characteristics of "Hedonic" happiness are that it is beyond our control and it never lasts long. This is the happiness that is the target of the quote by Joseph Epstein who said, "The good life has a great deal to do with contentment and satisfaction -- -- and nothing whatsoever to do with that fool's gold called happiness".

As humans we work very hard to accumulate "stuff". Money, fame, power, respect, more than our neighbors possess. Many work for those things because they think they will make them happy. But experience has shown us that whatever we accumulate will bring happiness only briefly. The answer of most to this problem is to try to get more. We believe that if we can get "enough" we will be happy despite the experience of our lives that there is never "enough". Scientific studies have shown that things beyond the necessities of life make little difference in the level of happiness.

We are afraid that if we give up now, all our efforts will have been in vain. That the major portion of our lives that we used to "get stuff" was a total waste. We would have to admit that the goal we were seeking was not the true goal. So we struggle on in the hope that the next level, more "stuff", will provide the longed for prize.

Another example of a misunderstanding about happiness (or perhaps the desire to look "smart" by knocking something that is popular) is the study by four academics that was excerpted in The Atlantic Magazine. The study concluded that the search for happiness was frivolous and self-centered. Only a life that had "meaning" could be truly worthwhile and satisfying.

The reason for the foolish conclusion became obvious when I looked at the original study and found that they had defined happiness as "getting what you want". I agree that getting what you want is a common goal but it will lead to happiness only if you want the right things.

Their conclusion assumed that happiness and meaning were mutually exclusive. Meaning can be one of the components of a happy life but every life with meaning is not necessarily happy.

Contrast these ideas and definitions of happiness with the observations of the Dalai Lama when he was asked, "What is the meaning of life?" a rather weighty question.

He answered immediately. "The meaning of life is happiness." He then added, "The hard question is not 'What is the meaning of life?' That is an easy question to answer. The hard question is 'What makes happiness? Money? Possessions? Accomplishments? Friends? Or .....compassion and a good heart? This is the question that all human beings must try to answer: What makes true happiness?"

True happiness is not the result of external factors but is an interior state of being. It is something we are, not something we do. We "be" happy. We do not "do" happy. It is a calmness of the soul. An acceptance of the life we are living and a joy in living it, both the things under our control and those that are not. Both the things we enjoy and those we don't. This is the happiness that is not fleeting but with us even when the world does not treat us as we think it should, when others don't do what we want, or do things that we don't want. It is the serenity of the soul that does not depend on external things beyond the necessities of life.

This is the happiness that Aristotle, Buddha, the Dalai Lama, and the psychologists, talk about. True happiness involves contentment, satisfaction, having challenge and the accomplishment of meeting it in our lives. It involves striving for a goal. It involves thinking of others and how our actions affect them. It means that we are doing our best, trying to actualize our incredible potential. It involves, as Aristotle said, living a life according to virtue.

It's all in how you look at it. Shakespeare said "Nothing is good or bad but thinking makes it so."

Centuries before Shakespeare, Epictetus said, "It's not what happens to you but how you react to it that matters."

Thoughts worth pondering.

I assume that you, dear reader, know when you are truly happy. Since none of us ever reach perfection, I assume that no matter how happy you are, you are interested in being even happier. I hope that you find this book helpful in your search.

JOYSONGS

I was once having a discussion about life with a Professor of English when he said, "John, you live your life by aphorism." He meant it as a demeaning comment. I looked up "aphorism" and found it defined as "A concise statement of a truth or principle". I should have thanked the Professor.

The following section contains aphorisms that I have found helpful in my pursuit of a happier life. There are many others. But these are the ones that I have found particularly helpful in facing life's common, everyday difficulties.

They hint at a way of viewing the world that cuts through the false barriers that we erect. The idea that we are separate. Or better than others. Or more perceptive. Or more aware.

If we are unhappy, perhaps it is not because of the world but the way we view it.

If we think that happiness is something over which we have little or no control, perhaps we are wrong.

Perhaps.

John Doherty

ENTHUSIASM IS THE MUSIC OF LIVING

Fear is the enemy of enthusiasm. The refusal to trust that life will continue to provide our needs in the future as it has in the past.

Enthusiasm is the ability to embrace life as it comes, seeking to experience its adventures rather than shrinking fearfully from imagined dangers.

Most of the things that happen to us can be enjoyable. The fears live mostly in our minds.

By living in the present we will be able to look on life as an adventure to be faced with enthusiastic anticipation, not something we must suffer through. Life is a difficult task, not necessarily a task we cannot enjoy.

Life has situations for us to overcome. Our enthusiasm should be for the adventure of the task rather than the satisfaction of the solution. Life is the process of participating, not the satisfaction of finishing.

Without enthusiasm, life is like a movie without music or food without seasoning.

Trust your experience. Put aside your fear.

Life is inevitable and exciting. How can it be faced with anything other than the spice of enthusiasm?

I CAN'T OR I WON'T

Fear and laziness often disguise themselves as helplessness. "I can't" often means that I am not willing to try. We are capable of far more than we will ever know. The capacity of every human is incredible and largely untapped.

One of the main reasons for this fear of trying is the emphasis in our society on goals; winning, and accomplishment. The goal of a game is not to win - it is to have fun. The reward is not in the score at the end but in the playing itself.

As T.S. Eliot said, "There is only the trying. The rest is not our concern."

Trying should be its own reward, not whether we accomplish our goal. Trying is totally within our control. Results are not.

When we turn our efforts to the joy of the attempt, we will be astonished at the results. We will learn that "I can't" is often just because we never tried.

John Doherty

PREFERENCES, NOT EXPECTATIONS

We would all prefer to be rich, strong, and good looking like the citizens of Lake Wobegon. But happiness suffers when the preference grows into expectation.

Because happiness cannot be seen or measured, society tries to apply other standards. It sets goals that define and measure "success". But those goals are generally wrong. Like measuring sound by the inch.

Expectations are limiting by definition. To have an expectation means that we cannot be happy unless we get what we expect.

Preferences are freeing. We can be happy without those things we would prefer to have.

Expectations doom us to disappointment for not all expectations can be met or fulfilled.

Preferences, by definition are not necessary.

Prefer whatever you want. But live your happy life without the expectation of ever getting it. The things you do receive will be better than the expectations of your imagination.

Don't limit your experience. Live it with openness rather than trying to push and pull it into the narrow confines of your "expectations".

HAPPINESS IS A STATE OF BEING

Happiness is a state of being. We do not desire to do happy but to be happy. We become happy simply by becoming happy. There are no prerequisites and there is no better time than NOW. Our happiness requires nothing that we do not already have.

Sound too good to be true? Are you one of those who believe that happiness is the result of something you will get? Do you wait for the opportunity each day to do or get the thing that will make you happy?

Your efforts will be unrewarded.

Money can buy comfort and comfort is nice. But happiness is far more desirable. We can claim our happiness anytime we choose. Just utilize the Eight Steps and see what a difference this change in outlook makes in your life.

Now is the time. With what you have. With who you are.

Why wait?

Claim it now. Be happy.

John Doherty

I AM WHO I AM,
NOT WHO I WAS, NOT WHO I WILL BE

I am a better, happier, more joyful and loving person than I was yesterday. Due to my efforts today, my positive traits will be even more developed tomorrow.

I am who I am. I accept that I have not yet arrived at perfection. Therefore, I will not have to lie and hide the true me from others. I relax in the comfort of accepting myself as I am today.

If I am not satisfied with the me that I am, then I can take steps today so that the me of tomorrow will better meet my expectations.

Just as I have the wonder of growth and discovery ahead of me, so too, others have the same experiences ahead of them. I will not rob them of those wonders by trying to change them.

Besides, I may be wrong.

I am who I am. I accept that I am not yet perfect. It is a job that I expect to be working on for the rest of my life.

The greatest creation of my life is me. I have not yet finished the job so hold your criticism until I'm done.

And I'll give you the same courtesy.

ALL THE IMPERFECT PEOPLE, PERFECTLY BEING THEMSELVES

No one is perfect - yet. Imperfection is the human condition we all share.

We have the right to demand that others accept our imperfection. We have the right to rebel when others hold us to their intolerable standards.

But this right imposes the duty to recognize that others are not perfect either. That they will as often fall short of our desires as we do of theirs. By accepting others as the beautiful, interesting, exciting people that they really are, we will no longer demand that they act as we judge best.

The excitement of people is in their unpredictable imperfection. By accepting this imperfection, we will be able to enjoy who people really are rather than trying to make them into pale copies of ourselves.

This attitude makes it easier for us not only to accept but to enjoy our own imperfection. The amazement when we ask, "Why the heck did I do that?" or, "Wow, I really did it, didn't I!" and especially, "Boy, was that a silly thing to do."

People don't have to be perfect. They don't have to be any better than they are. And neither do we.

You are perfectly, humanly imperfect. Relax and enjoy it!

John Doherty

FREEDOM OF RESPONSIBILITY, NOT FROM IT

Responsibility means that we accept the consequences of our actions. This acceptance guarantees freedom. Freedom from regrets that poison the present. Freedom from fear of the future. Freedom from the demands and judgments of others.

Many use what they call responsibility as a club to beat others into doing their will. To these people, responsibility means that you should do what they want. These are the ones who judge your past life, gladly pointing out what did not work.

They will cheerfully call you irresponsible for the mistakes you have made. They are blessed with 20-20 hindsight.

Once I accept responsibility for the failures and successes that are an inevitable part of living, and accept that I will have both in my experience, then the fear of the mistakes is lifted. I do not have to hide or deny them. I can accept them as part of experience.

For how would we know joy without pain, or heat without cold? The sweet is only sweet compared with the bitter. Success and failure are only names for opportunities to learn, for life experiences that went according to our desires or not.

Accepting all our actions allows us to be free to enjoy them all, not just the ones that have ended at the destination we chose.

I am responsible for all my choices. By accepting that responsibility I gain the freedom to be who I wish to be.

MY WAY

It is not only our right but our duty to live our lives as we see best. Certainly, each of us would take offense at others insisting that we do things their way. Why then are we so eager to tell others how to live their lives?

Why do we, whose lives are so far from perfection, seek to impose our solutions on others. Our unsought advice assumes that the other is too dense to see for him or herself what appears so clear to us.

In the arrogance of our imperfection, flying in the face of the evidence of our less than perfect lives, we dare to tell others how they should live.

Each problem is subject to many solutions. My answer is not necessarily the only one. Often, it is not even the best one.

John Doherty

WORRY

We humans are creatures addicted to worry. We worry about others with the excuse that the worry proves our love. We worry about the future as if it were in our control and pretend that it is the responsible thing to do. We worry about how others perceive us when it is one of the things over which we have no control at all.

Worry is a reaction to our fear of our inability to control things outside ourselves. It also makes happy living impossible.

Worry flies in the face of experience. Never in our lives has our worry done anything except make us miserable. All the worry in the world has never changed a single thing.

Only planning and action can affect change. Wasting energy worrying is an excuse for shirking our responsibility for action. It is an excuse for neglecting the real work of living; improving the happiness of our lives.

Worry is easier than the daunting task of living happily in a world over which we have little control. It is less than a waste of time. It is the enemy of happiness.

Use your experience. Accept that worry is useless. Stop it now!

DON'T BE RIGHT - JUST BE

Death is feared for it will finally take that thing we prize the most, life itself.

Our existence is far too precious a gift to waste. Just being is a major accomplishment. We should glory in the fact of being the wonderful creation that we are, the unknown capabilities that reside within us.

What a waste that we are taught we must follow paths that others tread. Many believe that their path is "right" as if there is only one acceptable way to live. We do not have to earn the right to explore our own path. That is a basic right which we have earned just by our existence.

There are many different paths in life and many yet untrodden. No one has the right to claim that theirs is the only one.

Do not seek the path you are told is "right". Seek rather to enjoy and explore the one on which you find yourself. Open your eyes to diversity. Allow others the right to live in their own way without imposing the false requirement that they meet your ideals.

Perhaps theirs are just as valid.

John Doherty

SILENCE IS GOLDEN

We hear it. We say it. We believe it. But how often do we practice it?

Many times the cacophony of our busy lives distracts us from the important job of truly living. Small concerns insist that they are of great importance. Time is filled with the mundane and our priorities become diverted from the true goal, happiness.

Many of these claims on our time are false. It is necessary to examine frequently how we are living and to review the goals for which we strive with so much effort. How easy to succumb to the claims of the unimportant and forget the major goal of our lives is our happiness.

It is said and generally ignored that "Silence is Golden". Silence provides us with the opportunity to examine our goals and to realign our priorities to achieve what is truly important

It has been foolishly said that "Winning is not the most important thing, it is the only thing".

Learning to live happily is the only thing. It honors the reason for our creation. It fulfills our potential. It nourishes our soul. A time of silence enables us to see the truly important.

ALL ALONE

Many people fear loneliness. Whether from fear of facing themselves or for other reasons does not matter. The idea that we are alone in the struggle of living is a fearful one. We are often alone but we need never be lonely.

But no one of us is really ever alone.

We are all one people, with the same instincts and desires.

Despite our different skin color, gender, or social standing we are all really far more alike than different.

The sameness extends far beyond the superficial similarities.

We are all part of creation. We share the precious gift of life, trying our best to spend it well.

We see only the outside of others. We cannot suspect what their inside looks like, but be assured, it is much like ours.

They have the same wants and needs as we. They, too, desire friends. They, too, need to give as well as receive. They, too, are afraid to expose themselves to being rebuffed if they offer the hand of friendship.

Only our fear, our opinion that others are different from ourselves, prevents the reaching out that establishes that human contact on which friendship, love, and sharing are based. The only reason for being alone is that we choose to be.

Most others are just as eager for contact with us as we are to contact them. The loneliness we fear is an illusion, easily dispersed with an outstretched hand.

John Doherty

SEEK THE RIGHT GOAL

Our "Primary Directive" is to seek happiness. It is the only goal we seek for itself. This is the goal that should direct all the other goals for which we strive.

Society sets goals that are commonly believed to bring happiness like money, fame, or power. Do not be deceived.

Go for happiness directly. The secondary goals that others present for us to achieve are false and unnecessary. Don't accept their promise.

Seek happiness itself, not one of its poor imitations.

Seek it with who you are.

With what you have.

Now.

"I AM WHO I AM.

THEY ARE WHO THEY ARE.

THE UNIVERSE IS AS IT IS.

THAT IS THE SECRET OF HAPPINESS."

Happiness is not an impossible goal. Each life can and should be happy.

Acceptance is one of the basic requirements for a happy life. Acceptance of three simple truths.

The first is acceptance of ourselves, the way we really are not the way we would like to be or the way we want others to think we are.

The second is the acceptance of others the way they really are; perfect in their human imperfection.

The third is the acceptance of the universe as it is.

By accepting these truths, we can enjoy ourselves, others, and the universe without improvement or change. We need wait for nothing to start being happy.

Now.

With who we are.

With what we have.

John Doherty

HAPPINESS IS BEING
IN THE RIGHT RELATIONSHIP
WITH THE UNIVERSE

The universe is a place of wonder for us to enjoy. The key to happiness is finding our proper place within it.

We don't need to fix it or others.

Promote honesty by being honest.

Promote love by loving.

Want what is.

Shun anger and the other negative emotions. Cast off guilt.

Live in the moment, sucking the reality from its bones before it becomes the dead past.

Enjoy the effort. Let the results take care of themselves.

Practice these principles constantly. On small things.

Go for happiness itself -- the only goal worthy of our effort.

Begin!

You Can B Happier Now

John Doherty

ABOUT THE AUTHOR

In 1984 John Doherty decided that Aristotle was right and that living happily was the goal of life. He then began the study and effort that showed that trying to live happily was work, and the harder you worked the more successful you would be. He also learned that trying to live a happy life required sharing, loving, kindness, and other ways of living that many call virtues.

He worked on Wall Street and in the financial industry for over 30 years. Since leaving the industry he built a home in a small town in New Hampshire. He enjoys hiking, gardening, talking with friends, and cooking for them. His cancer is under control and the deck he built looks out over a brook with a waterfall, Mt. Whiteface, and the 800,000 acres of the White Mountain National Forest.

Generally, but not always, he is happy.

CONNECT WITH JOHN

Glad you read my book and I hope you found it a helpful start on your journey to a happier life.

You can contact me at:

My Website: www.learningtobehappier.com

Email: www.zmurgy@gmail.com

Or even better, read my Blog at: www.happierlivingnow.blog.com

###

Made in the USA
Middletown, DE
29 July 2015